CW00872442

Does Racism Still Exist In America

Does Racism Still Exist In America

A Case Study

Dr. Forshaye Winbush

To order additional copies of this book, contact:
Xlibris
1-888-795-4274
www.Xlibris.com
Orders@Xlibris.com
546348

CONTENTS

This Book is dedicated to m my gifted Wife, Cecily Winbush, my Mother and Father Earline and Maurice, although they have passed, they handled Racism in such a way that we as a family and me and my siblings were able to adapt to how to recognize it and when to oppose it. Also to my daughters, Jamise, Essence, Morgan and Megan, and my grandchildren Zuri and Kaidance they are embracing a new racism that has been redefined and institutionalized and I hope and pray that they will oppose Racism with no fear. Love all of you. You all keep me on my GRIND every day. (Special thanks to Photographer Gregory, a dear friend of mine for taking the picture of me for this book).

FOREWORD

Some people may ask does racism truly exist in America still. After all we have had an American African as president. Well, let me explain to those who are wondering if racism still exist in America with the facts. The African American community since the first African that landed in Virginia as a slave, has had to fight racism in America for more than 400 years and we are still on the front lines fighting for our equal justice and our 40 acres and a mule which is now called reparations. You may remember roots written by Alex Haley. That story explains the existence of racism in America, get the book if you want to understand more, deeply how racism existed during slavery. In the 21st century Racism has been redefined because the act of enslaving American Africans has been redefined. Although we were supposedly emancipated, after reconstruction, Jim Crow and systemic racism started as soon as the emancipation proclamation was signed.

Racism is what American African have to deal with every day of their lives to survive in America. This country America, was built and developed and became prosperous because of the free labor bestowed upon Africans brought over here and enslaved for over 233 years and another 100 or so years Jim crow laws and now in the 21st century systemic racism. You see according to the constitution of the United States this country although stolen from the Indians is the Caucasoid man's country, via manifest destiny.

WHAT THE CONSTITUTION STATES

WE THE PEOPLE of the United States, to form a perfect Union, establish Justice, insure domestic Tranquility, provide for the common defense, promote the general Welfare, and secure the Blessings of Liberty to ourselves and our Posterity, do ordain and establish this Constitution for the United States of America.

My Interpretation of this statement above is, ourselves is saying for only white America. Because at the time this was written we were slaves considered non-human and chattel, like a cow. Then the constitution continues;

Representatives and direct Taxes shall be apportioned among the several States which may be included within this Union, according to their respective Numbers, which shall be determined by adding to the whole Number of free Persons, including those bound to Service for a Term of Years, and excluding Indians not taxed, three fifths of all other Persons.

Enslaved Africans were considered three-fifth of a person, and that was only added so that the southern states would be able to have more representatives in Congress because they did not want to get rid of slavery. This three-fifths statement is still written in the constitution and has not been removed. Which means to me that all American Africans are still considered three-fifths of a person and it takes five fifths to make a whole. Hmmm.'"

Now some may say what about the amendments, so let's address the amendments. These amendments were written after the Jim Crow laws were established that's why in the constitution, it means except as a punishment. So they had already established the fact that we were going to be arrested and jailed and outsourced yet again for free labor and these Jim Crow laws lasted for 100 years. So we were still excluded from the constitution as it was being written.

SECTION 1. Neither slavery nor involuntary servitude, except as a punishment for crime of which the party shall have been duly convicted, shall exist within the United States, or any place subject to their jurisdiction. **SECTION 2**. Congress shall have the power to enforce this article by appropriate legislation. **The amendment allowed all states specifically southern states to determine what**

they would do with their American Africans. Ushering in the end of reconstruction and the beginning of the Jim Crow laws. ARTICLE XIV. SECTION 1. All persons born or naturalized in the United States, and subject to the jurisdiction thereof, are citizens of the United States and the State wherein they reside – Except American Africans this article did not apply and does not really apply to this day systemic racism exist.

No State shall make or enforce any law which shall abridge the privileges or immunities of citizens of the United States; nor shall any State deprive any person of life, liberty, or property, without due process of law; nor deny to any person within its jurisdiction the equal protection of the laws.

All persons born or naturalized, again although most of us were born here through our ancestors that were brought over here as slaves we were not considered citizens of the good old U.S.A. because we were slaves. So yes this amendment was neglected and rejected by many states and Jim Crow laws and systemic racism was implemented to please those who still wanted slavery. So slavery would be redefined. And as it stands today systemic in the laws of America.

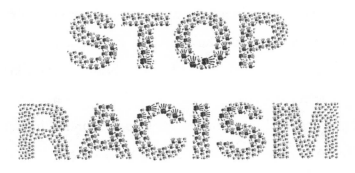

THE ORIGINS OF; JIM CROW

The roots of Jim Crow laws began as early as 1865, immediately after the ratification of the 13th amendment which outlawed slavery, "supposedly".

Jim Crow laws were a collection of laws that legalized racial segregation, which existed for 100 years from the post -Civil War era until 1968. These laws were meant to return Southern states back to slavery. These laws called Black codes were strict detailing laws that legally put American Africans into indentured servitude and took away voting rights, controlled where American Africans could live, how and when they could travel and even seized children for labor purposes. After slavery ended, many whites feared the freedom that American Africans had. They disliked the idea that it would be possible for American Africans to achieve the same social status as whites if given the equal access to employment, healthcare, housing, and education. (We have never been given these privileges not even to this day, why because of systemic Racism)

White America was already uncomfortable with the gains some American Africans made during Reconstruction, and took issue with such a prospect. As a result, states began to pass laws that placed some restrictions on American Africans. Collectively, these rules limited American Africans advancement and ultimately gave American Africans the status of second-class citizens, and deemed us inferior as they always had.

Racial apartheid in the United States soon earned the nickname, Jim Crow.

The moniker comes from a 19th-century minstrel song called "Jump Jim Crow," popularized by a minstrel performer named Thomas "Daddy" Rice, who appeared in blackface.

The Black Codes, according to History.com were a set of laws Southern states began passing in 1865, after slavery's end, and was a precursor to Jim Crow. The codes imposed curfews on blacks. Required unemployed blacks to be jailed and mandated that they get white sponsors to live in town or passes from their employers if they worked in agriculture.

The Black Codes even made it difficult for Americans Africans to hold meetings of any kind, including church services. American Africans who violated these laws could be fined, jailed, if they could not pay the fines, they were required to perform forced labor, just as they had while enslaved. Essentially, the codes recreated slavery.

Legislation such as the Civil Rights Act of 1866 and the Fourteenth and Fifteenth amendments sought to grant more liberties to American Africans. These laws, focused on citizenship and suffrage and did not prevent the enactment of Jim Crow laws.

Segregation did not only function to keep society racially segregated but also resulted in homegrown terrorism against American Africans. American Africans who did not obey Jim Crow laws could be beaten, jailed, maimed or lynched. Just as now we are jailed and killed by police officers, because of systemic racism.

Although an American African person needn't disobey Jim Crow laws to become a target of violent white racism. American African people who carried themselves with dignity, thrived economically, pursued education, dared to exercise their right to vote or rejected the sexual advances of whites could all be targets of white racism. In fact, an American African person needn't do anything at all to be victimized in this manner. If a white person just didn't like the look of an American African person, that American African could lose everything, including his or her life.

LEGAL CHALLENGES TO JIM CROW

The Supreme Court case Plessy v. Ferguson (1896) constituted the first major legal challenge to Jim Crow. The plaintiff in the case, Homer Plessy, a Louisiana Creole, was a shoemaker and activist who sat in a whites-only train car, for which he was arrested (as he and fellow activists planned). He fought his removal from the car all the way to the high court, which ultimately decided that "separate but equal" accommodations for blacks and whites weren't discriminatory.

Plessy, who died in 1925, would not live to see this ruling overturned by the landmark Supreme Court case Brown v. Board of Education (1954), which found that segregation was indeed discriminatory. Although this case focused on segregated schools, it led to the reversal of laws that enforced segregation in city parks, public beaches, public housing, interstate and intrastate travel and elsewhere.

Rosa Parks famously challenged racial segregation on city buses in Montgomery, Ala., when she refused to relinquish her seat to a white man on Dec. 1, 1955. Her arrest sparked the 381-day Montgomery Bus Boycott. While Parks challenged segregation on city buses, the activists known as the Freedom Riders challenged Jim Crow in interstate travel in 1961.

JIM CROW TODAY

Although racial segregation is illegal today, the United States continues to be a racially segregated society. Black and brown children are much more likely to attend schools with other black and brown children than they are with whites. Schools today are, in fact, more segregated than they were in the 1970s.

Similarly, laws that target undocumented immigrants such as the Georgia Law SB350 have led to the introduction of the term "Juan Crow." Anti-immigrant bills such as SB 54, passed in states such as California, Arizona, and Alabama in recent decades have resulted in unauthorized immigrants living in the shadows, subject to poor working conditions, predatory landlords, a lack of healthcare, sexual assault, domestic violence and more. Sounds like slavery.

Although some of these laws have been struck down or primarily gutted, their passage in various states has created a hostile climate that makes undocumented immigrants feel dehumanized.

Jim Crow is a ghost of what it once was, but racial divisions continue to characterize American life. Although we have had and American African President Barack Obama. The new Jim Crow is a rebirth of a system that has made the majority of American African men permanent second class citizens with no rights because of the massive incarceration that takes place in America against American African males.

FAILED INTEGRATION

In the 21st century systemic racism still separates us today, by laws. Except that now, we have no place to call our own, there is no black wall, street or communities controlled by American Africans such as Harlem, New York was, once upon a time. So I ask was integration really worth what we suffer through today. Fifteen years after Brown vs Board the United States is still as segregated as it was before the 21st century. While in the abstract we would like to believe that the United States of America is integrated, the reality is that it is not. According to Sheryll Cashin author of the Failures of Integration, a *New York Times* poll on racial attitudes: 85 percent of whites said in response to a poll question that they did not care whether they lived in an area where most of their neighbors were white or where most were black; but in response to another question, 85 percent of whites also said they actually live in areas where they have no or few black neighbors. The majority of Americans say they support integration. But this is not the reality that the majority of us actually live. Most of us do not share life space with other races or classes. And we do not own up to the often gaping inequality that results from this separation because, being physically removed from those who most suffer the costs of separatism, we cannot acknowledge what we don't see, because we do not want to see them.

Even as our nation diversifies at a rapid pace, we are haunted by old standards and old ways of thinking. In 1954, about 87 percent of the population was white, 10 percent was black, and the small remainder was composed of Latinos, Asians, and Native Americans. Our national struggle with race relations was between that of black and white. The fear toward integration of black people into white neighborhoods and white institutions colored how America came to be ordered. The predictable patterns of urban concentration of blacks and the minority poor and suburban concentrations of whites and the affluent emerged through the consciousness of public policies and a great deal of discrimination against black people. America felt as though they had a "Negro problem."

Five decades later, our nation is infinitely more diverse; Latinos now outnumber African Americans and we are headed toward a new social order. By the end of the new century, we will be a majority-minority nation with whites composing only 40 percent of the national population. American separatism, however, endures, and its class dimensions seem to be growing. We have not yet figured out how to break out of separatist patterns burnished in less enlightened times, and we rarely, if ever, have any explicit discourse about it.

Ironically, while the nation has not yet moved beyond a fundamental hurdle regarding integration, the discomfort of many with large numbers of black people which are some of the most admired and respected national figures in the United States are black. White America embraces Colin Powell, Oprah Winfrey, Tiger Woods. They admire Michael Jordan, Condoleezza Rice. There are enough examples of successful middleclass American Africans to make many whites believe that blacks have reached equality with them. The fact that some blacks now lead powerful mainstream institutions offers evidence to whites that racial barriers have been eliminated; the issue now is individual effort. In December 2001, when Richard Parsons, an African American, was named the CEO of AOL Time Warner, then the largest media company in the world, it was not an earth-shattering event. Not much was made of the fact that President George W. Bush chose a black woman, Condoleezza Rice, to head his National Security Council or that Colin Powell was the first black Secretary of State. As a nation we seem to have moved past the era when the "first black" is noted, celebrated, or even explicitly discussed. For many, if not most, whites, words like "segregation" and "inequality" are old, finished business. And words like "integration" and "affirmative action" are beyond the point. Whites are now tired of black complaints because they are rather misinformed about how well African Americans are doing. Depending on the question, in response to opinion polls, between 40 and 60 percent of whites say that blacks are doing as well as, if not better than, they are in terms of jobs, incomes, education, and access to health care. No doubt, American Africans have progressed, but the closing of social and economic gaps is in the minds of white Americans. According to a recent surveys, half of whites believe that the average black person is as well off as the average white person in terms of employment, even though blacks are about twice as likely as whites to hold lower-paying service jobs and more than twice as likely to be unemployed. Four in ten whites incorrectly believed that the typical black earned as much as or more than the typical white, even though black median household income is about 64 percent that of whites—$29,500 compared to $46,300 for whites. (The disparity in terms of wealth, as opposed to income, is much worse: Black median wealth is about 16 percent that of whites.) There were similar gaps of perception and reality concerning education and health care. The odd black family on the block or the Oprah effect—examples of stratospheric black success, feed these misperceptions, even as relatively few whites live among and interact daily with blacks of their own social standing. We are still quite far from the integrated, equal opportunity nation whites seem to think we have become.

Black people, on the other hand, have become integration weary. Most African Americans do not crave integration, although they support it. What seems to matter most to black people is not living in a well-integrated neighborhood but having the same access to the good things in life as everyone else. There is much evidence of an emerging "post, civil rights" attitude among black folks. We are uncertain integrationists. In opinion polls, the majority of American Africans say that they would prefer to live in an integrated neighborhood, but for some of us integration now means a majority-black neighborhood, a neighborhood where you are not overwhelmed by white people and where there are plenty of your own kind around to make you feel comfortable, supported, and welcome. Across America, wherever there is a sizeable black middle-class population, suburban black enclaves have cropped up that attest to the draw of this happy "we" feeling.

This is not separatism in the classic sense. Black people want the benefits of an integrated workplace; we want the public and private institutions that shape opportunity to be integrated. More fundamentally, we want the freedom to chart our course and pursue our dreams. We bang on the doors and sometimes shatter the ceilings of corporate America not because it is largely white but because this is how to "get paid." We want an integrated commercial sector because we want banks and venture capitalists to lend to us and invest in our business ideas. We want the option of sending our children to any college we desire but for many of us Howard, Morehouse, or any number of historically black colleges are at the top of our list. We want space on the airwaves for our music, preferably aired by black-owned radio stations. We want space in Hollywood and on the big screen for our films. We want to see and celebrate ourselves on television, but we do not particularly care that there was not a black friend on "Friends;" most of us didn't watch it and didn't understand its appeal.

Even at the height of the civil rights era, socializing with whites was never a goal in itself for black people, and undoubtedly for many, it is not one today. There are counter examples, but we all know they are fairly rare. For those blacks, like myself, who attended primarily white schools, the dominant pattern of socialization was that blacks hung with blacks. And at most social gatherings that I attended then and those that I attend now, one race overwhelmingly predominates. Even when I attend functions that might be described as well integrated, I often observe the phenomenon of blacks pairing with blacks and whites paring with whites. Obviously there are exceptions. I am necessarily writing about generalities. But these generalities reflect certain truths, typically unspoken ones about the limits of integration in our nation. I also have been the only American African that worked for a company or the only American African that worked in a certain department for a major company. And I always felt the pressure of representing for my people, feeling as though I was an experiment for the company to determine if they would hire other American Africans. I am absolutely positive that we as a people are the only ones who deal with this type of pressure while we are on a corporate and or any job. This feeling stems from the fact that I was taught you have to be ten times better than they are and in being ten and sometimes twenty times better than they are you are still punished for the color of your skin.

INSTITUTIONAL RACISM

Institutional racism (also known as institutionalized/ Systemic racism) is a form of racism expressed in the practice of social and political institutions. Institutional racism is also racism by individuals or informal social groups, governed by behavioral norms that support racist thinking and instigates actual racism. It is reflected in disparities regarding wealth, income, criminal justice, employment, housing, healthcare, political power, and education, among other things. Whether implicitly or explicitly expressed, institutional racism occurs when a particular group is targeted and discriminated against based on race or the color of their skin. Institutional racism is mostly implicit so it goes unnoticed frequently; this is why it is overlooked. Institutional racism was explained in 1967 by Kwame Ture (Formerly Stokely Carmichael) and Charles V. Hamilton in Black Power: The Politics of Liberation, stating that while individual racism is often identifiable because of its open nature, institutional racism is less perceptible because of its "less overt, far more subtle" nature. Institutional racism "originates in the operation of established and respected forces in the society, and thus receives far less public condemnation than [individual racism]." They go on to give examples:

"When white terrorists bomb a black church and kill five black children that is an act of individual racism, widely deplorable by most segments of the society. But when in that same city--Birmingham, Alabama--five hundred black babies die each year because of the lack of power, food, shelter and medical facilities, and thousands more are destroyed and maimed physically, emotionally and intellectually because of conditions of poverty and discrimination in the black community, that is a function of institutional racism. When a black family moves into a home in a white neighborhood and is stoned, burned or routed out, they are victims of an overt act of individual racism which most people will condemn. But it is institutional racism that keeps black people living in dilapidated slum tenements, subject to the daily prey of exploitative slumlords, merchants, loan sharks and discriminatory real estate agents. The society either pretends it does not know of these latter situation or is, in fact, incapable of doing anything meaningful about it." And let's not forget how we are shot down in the streets and killed by police officers who feel threaten by black men of any shape age or size.

Institutional racism was defined by Sir William Macpherson in the 1999 Lawrence report (UK) as: "The collective failure of an organization to provide an appropriate and professional service to people because of their color, culture, or ethnic origin. It can be seen or detected in processes, attitudes, and behaviors which amount to discrimination through unwitting prejudice, ignorance, thoughtlessness and racist stereotyping which disadvantage minority ethnic people.

HOW POLITICS IS A MAJOR FACTOR IN HOW RACISM IS VIEWED IN AMERICA

The most significant crime in the U.S. criminal justice system is that it is a race-based institution where African-Americans are directly targeted and punished in a much more aggressive way than white people.

Saying the US criminal system is racist may be politically controversial in some circles. But the facts are overwhelming. No real debate about that. Below I set out numerous examples of these circumstances.

The question is – are these facts the mistakes of an otherwise sound system, or are they evidence that the racist criminal justice system is working exactly as intended? Is the US criminal justice system operated to marginalize and control millions of African Americans?

Information on race is available for each step of the criminal justice system – from the use of drugs, police stops, getting out on bail, legal representation, jury selection, trial, sentencing, prison, parole, and freedom. Look what these facts show.

One. The US has seen a surge in arrests and putting people in jail over the last four decades. Most of the reason is the war on drugs. Whites and blacks engage in drug offenses, possession, and sales, at roughly comparable rates – according to a report on race and drug enforcement published by Human Rights Watch in May 2008. While African Americans comprise 13% of the US population and 14% of monthly drug users they are 37% of the people arrested for drug offenses – according to 2009 Congressional testimony by Marc Mauer of The Sentencing Project.

Two. The police stop blacks and Latinos at rates that are much higher than whites. In New York City, where people of color make up about half of the population, 80% of the NYPD stops were of blacks and Latinos. When whites were stopped, only 8% were frisked. When blacks and Latinos are stopped, 85% were searched according to information provided by the NYPD.

The same is true most other places as well. In a California study, the ACLU found blacks are three times more likely to be stopped than whites.

Three. Since 1970, drug arrests have skyrocketed rising from 320,000 to close to 1.6 million according to the Bureau of Justice Statistics of the U.S. Department of Justice. African Americans are arrested for drug offenses at rates 2 to 11 times higher than the rate for whites – according to a May 2009 report on disparity in drug arrests by Human Rights Watch.

Four. Once arrested, blacks are more likely to remain in prison awaiting trial than whites. For example, the New York state division of criminal justice did a 1995 review of disparities in processing felony arrests and found that in some parts of New York blacks are 33% more likely to be detained awaiting felony trials than whites facing felony trials.

Five. Once arrested, 80% of the people in the criminal justice system get a public defender for their lawyer. Race plays a big role here as well. Stop in any urban courtroom and look at the color of the people who are waiting for public defenders. Despite often heroic efforts by public defenders, the system gives them much more work and much less money than the prosecution. The American Bar Association, reviewed the US public defender system in 2004 and concluded "All too often, defendants plead guilty, even if they are innocent, without really understanding their legal rights or what is occurring. The fundamental right to a lawyer that America assumes applies to everyone accused of criminal conduct effectively does not exist in practice for countless people across the US."

Especially African Americans, because we are not considered to be Americans, so therefore we have no rights.

Six. African Americans are frequently illegally excluded from criminal jury service according to a June 2010 study released by the Equal Justice Initiative.

For example in Houston County, Alabama, 8 out of 10 African Americans qualified for jury service have been struck by prosecutors from serving on death penalty cases. Maybe it is because we are more apt to be skeptical of what is presented by police, because in our community they do not always tell the truth.

Seven. Trials are rare. Only 3 to 5 percent of criminal cases go to trial – the rest are plea bargained. Most African Americans defendants never get a trial. Most plea bargains consist of the promise of a longer sentence if a person exercises their constitutional right to trial. As a result, people caught up in the system, as the American Bar Association points out, plead guilty even when innocent. Why? As one young man told me recently, "Who wouldn't rather do three years for a crime they didn't commit than risk twenty-five years for a crime they didn't do?" and considering we are already found guilty by just being black. We are scared and we know the justice system is not designed for our justice.

Eight. The U.S. Sentencing Commission reported in March 2010 that in the federal system black offenders receive sentences that are 10% longer than white offenders for the same crimes. Marc Mauer of the Sentencing Project reports African Americans are 21% more likely to receive mandatory minimum sentences than white defendants and 20% more likely to be sentenced to prison than white drug defendants. Still enslaved for free labor.

Nine. The longer the sentence, the more likely it is that non-white people will be the ones getting it. A July 2009 report by the Sentencing Project found that two-thirds of the people in the US with life sentences are non-white. In New York, it is 83%.

Ten. As a result, African Americans, who are 13% of the population and 14% of drug users, are not only 37% of the people arrested for drugs but 56% of the people in state prisons for drug offenses. Marc Mauer May 2009 Congressional Testimony for The Sentencing Project.

Eleven. The US Bureau of Justice Statistics concludes that the chance of a black male born in 2001 of going to jail is 32% or 1 in three. Latino males have a 17% chance, and white males have a 6% chance. Thus black boys are five times and Latino boys nearly three times as likely as white boys to go to jail. We are lost before we are even born, God help us.

Twelve. So, while African American juvenile youth is but 16% of the population, they are 28% of juvenile arrests, 37% of the youth in juvenile jails and 58% of the youth sent to adult prisons. 2009 Criminal Justice Primer, the Sentencing Project.

Thirteen. Remember that the US leads the world in putting American Africans in jail and prison. The New York Times reported in 2008 that the US has five percent of the world's population but a quarter of the world's prisoners, over 2.3 million people behind bars, dwarfing other nations. The US rate of incarceration is five to eight times higher than other highly developed countries, and black males are the largest percentage of inmates according to an ABC News report on incarceration.

Fourteen. Even when released from prison, race continues to dominate. A study by Professor Devah Pager of the University of Wisconsin found that 17% of white job applicants with criminal records received call backs from employers while only 5% of black job applicants with criminal records received call backs. The race is so prominent in that study that whites with criminal records received better treatment than blacks without criminal records. So, what conclusions do these facts lead to? The criminal justice system, from start to finish, is seriously racist.

Professor Michelle Alexander concludes that it is no coincidence that the criminal justice system ramped up its processing of African Americans just as the Jim Crow laws enforced since the age of slavery ended.

Her book, The New Jim Crow: Mass Incarceration in the Age of Colorblindness sees these facts as evidence of the new way the USA has decided to control African Americans – a racialized system of social control. The stigma of criminality functions in much the same way as

Jim Crow – creating legal boundaries between them and us, allowing legal discrimination against us, removing the right to vote from millions, and essentially warehousing a disposable population of unwanted people. She calls it a new caste system. Poor whites and people of other ethnicity are also subjected to this system of social control. Because if poor whites or others get out of line, they will be given the worst possible treatment, they will be treated just like poor blacks.

Other critics like Professor Dylan Rodriguez see the criminal justice system as a key part of what he calls the domestic war on the marginalized. Because of globalization, he argues in his book Forced Passages; that there is an excess of people in the USA and elsewhere. "These people," whether they are in Guantanamo or Abu Ghraib or US jails and prisons, are not productive, are not needed, are not wanted and are not entitled to the same human rights as the productive ones. They must be controlled and dominated for the safety of the productive. They must be intimidated into accepting their inferiority, or they must be removed from the society of the productive.

This domestic war relies on the same technology that the US uses internationally. More and more we see the militarization of this country's police. Likewise, the goals of the US justice system are the same as the US war on terror - domination and control by capture, immobilization, punishment, and liquidation.

WHAT AMERICAN AFRICANS CAN TO DO TO HELP GET RID OF RACISM IN AMERICA

Martin Luther King Jr. said we as a nation must undergo a radical revolution of values. A radical approach to the US criminal justice system means we must go to the root of the problem. Not reform. Not better beds in better prisons. We are not called to only trim the leaves or prune the branches, but rip up this unjust system by its roots, and radically change it.

We are all entitled to safety. That is a human right everyone has a right to expect. But do we think that continuing with a deeply racist system leading the world in incarcerating our children is making us safer?

It is time for every person interested in justice and safety to join in and dismantle this racist system. Should the US decriminalize drugs like marijuana? Should prisons be abolished? Should we expand the use of restorative justice? Can we create fair educational, medical and employment systems? All these questions and much more have to be seriously explored. We should all be doing something such as joining a group like INCITE, Critical Resistance, the Center for Community Alternatives, The national Action Network, Thousand Kites, or any church and we should be involved and work in these organizations to bring about the changes that are needed in America. As Professor Alexander says "Nothing short of a major social movement can dismantle this new caste system.

According to Danyelle Solomon; vice president of Race and Ethnicity Policy at the center for American Progress. For centuries, the country and its economic base were fueled by the bodies of slaves and indigenous people, who were mined, exploited, and sold in order to build the world's most powerful economic system. For more than 200 years, a permanent system of exploitation, deprivation, and murder persisted that was justified by race. Validated by an ideology of white supremacy and accompanied by a narrative of racial difference and "othering," Black Americans were deprived of all rights and autonomy.[4] The institution of slavery yielded more than $14 trillion dollars and laid the groundwork for the concentration of wealth and power in the hands of white Americans.[5] It was so powerful and lucrative that the United States went to war with itself to preserve it.[6]

The abolishment of slavery at the end of the Civil War upended an economic system that threatened the economic well-being of white Americans and their heirs. Wealth, the best economic indicator of a person or family's overall well-being, is typically gained through the collection of assets, such as land and money.[7] Not only did the end of slavery mean the end of "free labor" but it also brought about Reconstruction and the redistribution of wealth. During a meeting with then-Secretary of War Edwin McMasters Stanton and Union Gen. William T. Sherman in 1865, a group of Black Baptist and Methodist ministers discussed the importance of land. For them, freedom was "placing [them] where [they] could reap the fruit of [their] own labor."[8] Following the meeting, Gen. Sherman issued Special Field Order No. 15, which instructed the federal government to redistribute 40-acre plots of land to the newly freed slaves so that they could create a life for themselves.[9] This redistribution of wealth was significant because it was meant to upend the current way of life; as President Abraham Lincoln once said, "Reconstruction is more difficult and dangerous than construction or destruction."[10]

What is important to recognize about that moment in United States' history is that policymakers used the opportunity to correct a wrong and rebuild the nation. They took the steps to provide "seed capital" to the Black Americans who built the country. And with the passage of the 14th and 15th amendments, Black Americans secured citizenship and the right to participate in the democratic process. They were even elected to the U.S. Congress.[11] But the evergreen toxin of racism would not allow for progress to continue. The redistribution of wealth during Reconstruction lasted less than a year; in 1865, the land was returned to former white slaveowners.[12]

Furthermore, the wealth that white families gained during slavery was passed down from generation to generation, compounding and growing over time. And while the system of subjugating and exploiting African Americans was modified by policy and practices, it continued—and its effects compounded over time. Slavery was followed by decades of terror and exclusion in all aspects of American life;[13] it provided the scaffolding and paved the way for decades of intentional, systematic disenfranchisement of African Americans. It provided a reference point for the exclusionary language found in government programs, such as the GI Bill and Federal Housing Administration (FHA) loans, that blocked Black Americans from the home and student loan programs that helped build the middle class.[14] Slavery also provided a reference point for practices such as redlining and blockbusting, which stoked fear among white people of living near black neighbors. In short, slavery was the basis upon which the United States continued to systematically and deliberately undervalue the work, humanity, and abilities of Black Americans.

400 YEARS OF COLLECTIVE HARM

This collective impact of efforts to undervalue Black Americans has yielded the disparities seen today: White Americans have 10 times the wealth of Black Americans; Black women die in childbirth at three to four times the rate of white women; and 1 in 3 Black men will likely enter the criminal justice system at some point during their lifetime. Additionally, nearly 1 in 5 Black Americans have experienced some form of voter suppression in their lifetimes.[18] These outcomes sprout from the soil of the nation's founding. Today, centuries since the first slave ships came to Virginia, America has a unique opportunity to finally institute a plan of action that atones for the sins of slavery and corrects centuries of emotional, economic, and physical harm. This "truth and reconciliation" plan will break the reference point of slavery and replace it with an intentional choice to do the hard work to rebuild itself in an equitable manner. The U.S. government must make the intentional choice to finally and fully correct 400 years of collective harm.

One of the most effective ways to address this collective harm is to tackle the racial wealth gap. Wealth allows people to move through life seamlessly. It allows people to purchase a home, respond to an emergency, or put their children through college. It is the inheritance received and passed down through generations. White Americans have 10 times the wealth of Black Americans not only because they inherited what their ancestors gained from slavery, but also because they benefited from the policies and practices that followed. Even when controlling for protective factors such as education, income, and homeownership, Black Americans still have significantly less wealth than their white counterparts.[19] In 1860, Jefferson Davis, then a senator from Mississippi and the soon-to-be president of the Confederate States of America, said that the U.S. system of government was not "founded by negroes nor for negroes," but "by white men for white men."[20] Therefore, the inequality seen today should not be surprising, and Americans should instead understand that it was "stamped from the beginning."[21]

CONCLUSION

As policymakers and presidential nominees engage in conversations about systematic inequality, they must be bold; they must be honest; they must deliver intentional and targeted approaches. This moment—a moment in which 84 percent of Black Americans and 58 percent of white Americans believe that the legacy of slavery affects the current outcomes for black people must be used to make real structural change. Policymakers must support H.R. 40, a bill that would support studying the impact of slavery on present-day outcomes. They must also support and analyze reparations as a possible policy intervention for closing the racial wealth gap because the sheer volume of harms, combined with the compounding impact over 400 years, makes it hard to justify not doing so.

For the United States to move toward real equality, it must work toward "the full acceptance of our collective biography and its consequences. Only then will the nation successfully right an unjustifiable wrong and fundamentally change an economic and social system built on suppression and the concentration of wealth and power.

REFERENCES

Bill Quigley - Associate Director of the Center for Constitutional Rights and a law professor at Loyola University New Orleans.
quigley77@gmail.com

Danyelle Solomon is the vice president of Race and Ethnicity Policy at the Center for American Progress.

Samantha Wolk - Senior Legal Assistant of CAP and CAP Action
https://www.americanprogress.org/issues/courts/news/2005/06/15/1497/the-failures-of-integration/

https://www.americanprogress.org/issues/race/reports/2019/08/07/472899/truth-and-reconciliation/

Sheryll Cashill – The Failure of Integration

Dr. Martin Luther King Jr (Autobiography Alex Haley)
Malcolm X Quotes – Brainy Quotes
https://www.brainyquote.com/authors/malcolm_x

Professor Dylan Rodriguez (Prison /Genocide/Abolition – (book forced Passages)

Professor Michelle Alexander

The Origins of Jim Crow (Ferris State University Big rapids Michigan)

The Jim Crow era by Femi Lewis

The Civil Rights Act of 1964 Did Not End the Movement For Equality By Lisa Vox

The Reconstruction Era (1865–1877) By Robert Mcnamara

United States Constitution

https://www.opendemocracy.net/en/14-shocking-facts-that-prove-us-criminal-justice-system-is-racist/

https://www.thoughtco.com/what-is-the-definition-of-jim-crow-laws-2834618

https://en.wikipedia.org/wiki/Institutional racism

CPSIA information can be obtained
at www.ICGtesting.com
Printed in the USA
BVHW031116210120
569972BV00035B/53/J